Dick Bruna

The Orchestra

Dick Bruna Books, Inc.
PRICE/STERN/SLOAN
Publishers, Inc., Los Angeles
1984

We are eleven players—

an orchestra we form.

We play a lot together

and joyfully perform.

Susanna plays upon the flute

which has a silvery shine.

It is long and thin and graceful.

The sound it makes is fine.

Cathy plays the recorder—

a wooden pipe that is round

with little cut holes in it.

It makes a wooden sound.

Ben blows on the trumpet.

His cheeks get very round.

He can play it very softly

or make an elephant sound.

Beth is the violinist.

She is very good, you know.

You ought to hear her playing

just how the notes should go.

Susan plays the cello.

Although the cello stands,

she has to sit to play it

to reach it with her hands.

The double bass is Peter's.

It is the biggest of them all.

You have to stand to play it

even if you are very tall.

Penny plays the piano.

She sits down on the seat

to play the keyboard with her hand

the pedals with her feet.

Then there is Jerry.

The guitar that he brings

has not just three or four or five

but, count them all, six strings!

A harp has many more strings.

Jessica plays so well

that she can make them sing and shiver

or tinkle like a bell.

Bob plays percussion

with every kind of drum.

He hits the snare and cymbals, too,

with a rum-ti-ti-tum-tum-tum.

The conductor's name is Michael.

He has to set the pace.

He keeps his eye on all of us,

but you don't see his face.

Eleven are in our orchestra.

Our music is all the rage.

If you want to see us play,

simply turn the page.

Books by Dick Bruna:

First published in the U.S.A. 1984
by Dick Bruna Books Inc., New York
Illustrations Dick Bruna
Copyright Mercis bv., Amsterdam © 1984, all rights reserved
Text copyright © Dick Bruna 1984
Exclusively arranged and produced by Mercis Publishing bv., Amsterdam
Printed and bound by Brepols Fabrieken nv., Turnhout, Belgium
I.S.B.N. 0-8431-1529-7